SPORTING SKILLS

TAEKWONDO

CLIVE GIFFORD

Published in 2013 by Wayland

Copyright © Wayland 2013

Wayland
Hachette Children's Books
338 Euston Road
London NW1 3BH

Wayland Australia
Level 17/207 Kent Street
Sydney, NSW 2000

Editorial Director: Rasha Elsaeed

Produced by Tall Tree Ltd
Editor: Jon Richards
Designer: Ben Ruocco
Photographer: Michael Wicks

British Library Cataloguing in Publication Data

Gifford, Clive.
   Taekwondo. -- (Sporting skills)
   1. Tae kwon do--Juvenile literature.
   I. Title II. Series
   796.8'153-dc22

ISBN: 9780750278669

10 9 8 7 6 5 4 3 2 1

Printed in China

Wayland is a division of Hachette Children's
Books, an Hachette UK company.
www.hachette.co.uk

Picture credits
All photographs taken by Michael Wicks,
except;
5 Ezra Shaw/Getty Images, 27 tr courtesy of
J. K. Lee Black Belt Academy and Scott D.
Feldstein, 29 br Quinn Rooney/Getty Images

Acknowledgements
The author and publisher would like to thank
the following people for their help and
participation in this book:
St Albans LTSI (www.uk-ltsi.com)
Coach: Chris Snow 5th Degree ITF
Jade Doran, Hamish Jeram, Rishi Magudia,
Lauren Snow and Rhiannon Snow

The website addresses (URLs) included in this
book were valid at the time of going to press.
However, because of the nature of the
Internet, it is possible that some addresses
may have changed, or sites may have changed
or closed down, since publication. While the
author and Publisher regret any inconvenience
this may cause the readers, no responsibility
for any such changes can be accepted by
either the author or the Publisher.

Disclaimer
In preparation of this book, all due care has
been exercised with regard to the advice,
activities and techniques depicted. The
publishers regret that they can accept no
liability for any loss or injury sustained.
When learning a new sport it is important
to get expert tuition and to follow a
manufacturer's instructions.

In this book, we have used different
coloured arrows to show the movement of
the body and different body parts. A red
arrow shows movement of the whole body,
while a blue arrow shows the movement of
a body part, such as the arms.

CONTENTS

WHAT IS TAEKWONDO?

Taekwondo is a martial art that started out in Korea and is now practised by more than 60 million students worldwide.

TAKING PART

Taekwondo means the 'art of foot and hand fighting' or the 'way of the foot and fist'. Taekwondo includes many hand and arm movements, such as punches, but unlike some other martial arts, it places emphasis on kicks or strikes with the feet.

There are a number of different styles of taekwondo, but all are suitable for boys and girls to learn as well as adults. There are also different reasons why people get into this popular martial art. A small number progress to fighting opponents in competitions called bouts. Many people take up taekwondo for the challenge of learning the moves and to build up their strength, speed, balance and flexibility. Others learn taekwondo as a method of self-defence.

DID YOU KNOW?

During the Korean Si Dynasty (1392–1910), flying kicks were developed in Korea that historians believe were used to knock riders off their horses!

Taekwondo sessions can be very demanding and they are a good way of improving a person's fitness.

This taekwondo class is practising some moves, with the pupils performing punches, blocks and kicks all at the same time.

4

A LONG HISTORY

Many people believe taekwondo developed more than 2,000 years ago from ancient Korean fighting techniques. It may also have been influenced by Japanese martial arts as Japan occupied Korea from 1910 to 1945. After Japanese occupation ended, a version of the sport was made a part of training in the Korean military forces. In 1955, the many different experts in the sport met in Korea, where it was made the country's national sport. Taekwondo schools started to spring up in Asia, Europe and the United States. In 1973, the World Taekwondo Federation (WTF) held the first ever world championships, and 15 years later, in 1988, taekwondo made its debut at the Olympics. Today, the two biggest organizations running taekwondo around the world are the WTF and the International Taekwondo Federation (ITF). Each of these has its own rules for competitions (see page 28). The moves shown in this book follow ITF guidelines.

Know your numbers

In taekwondo classes, moves and timings may be given by the instructor using numbers in the Korean language, so it is a good idea to learn numbers up to ten.

hanah = one
dool = two
set = three
net = four
dasot = five
yasot = six
ilgob = seven
yadol = eight
ahop = nine
yool = ten

Dongmin Cha of Korea (in red) tries to kick Akmal Irgashev of Uzbekistan (in blue) during the 2008 Olympic Games in Beijing, China.

CLOTHING AND BELTS

Taekwondo is performed wearing an all-white uniform called a dobok. This consists of trousers, which are put on first, with a loose jacket worn over the upper body. The jacket is tied using a special belt.

STARTING OUT

When you first visit a taekwondo school and take an introduction class or session, you are likely to be asked to wear a T-shirt and tracksuit bottoms. As you progress, you will wear your own dobok uniform, which can be bought through your taekwondo school. The dobok is made from heavy cotton. It is comfortable to wear and should be well looked after and kept cleaned and ironed between sessions.

This student is wearing her white dobok. Her hands and feet are clean and her hair has been tied back to keep it out of her eyes. Her toenails and fingernails will be cut short so that they do not scratch another student.

The belt

Belts are colour-coded to show the level of the student. As a beginner you will wear a white belt. As you learn more moves and pass grading exams, you will progress to yellow, green, blue, red and finally black. The belt should be tied in the correct way, as shown in the sequence below.

SAFETY FIRST

Like many martial arts, taekwondo has rules to keep you safe. For example, all watches and jewellery should be removed before taking part and moves should never be practised on others outside of your class. When sparring (practising moves with another student), you will usually wear protective equipment. The type of protective padding you wear will depend on the style of taekwondo taught by your school. It can include a chest protector, gloves, overshoes and a headguard, all of which are padded to provide protection. A mouthguard to protect your teeth is also recommended.

Target pads

You will use special pads called target or focus pads to practise kicks and punches. Here, a student is practising an axe kick (see page 19) while another student holds a small target pad.

This student has put on her protective equipment, ready to spar with another martial artist at an ITF school. She is wearing padded gloves and overshoes, a padded headguard and a mouthguard. If her school were part of the WTF, she would also wear pads on her upper body.

IN THE DOJANG

Most taekwondo training takes place in a martial arts school, which is known as a dojang. Students are expected to arrive on time for their class and show respect to their dojang by performing a bow called kyong ye as they enter or leave.

GETTING READY

Students begin each taekwondo session with a period of preparation to get their minds and bodies ready for the effort ahead. This preparation involves gentle exercises to warm up, such as jogging, and sometimes more vigorous movements, such as push-ups, sit-ups and star jumps. Taekwondo sessions often include intense physical exercise with sharp movements of the arms and legs. This is why muscles need to be stretched beforehand to avoid injuries.

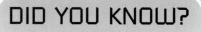

DID YOU KNOW?

In 2009, the very first World Para-Taekwondo Championships were held in Azerbaijan for competitors with disabilities. People from 16 countries took part.

This student is bowing as she enters the dojang at the start of a lesson.

Here, a student and teacher are bowing to each other. The student will start the bow and the teacher then bows in reply.

Talking taekwondo

Many terms for objects and actions in taekwondo are in the Korean language. Here are some common words you might hear in a dojang.

ho shin sul – self-defence
si jak – start
gomman – stop
charyot – watch
gyesok – continue
dwirro torra – turn around
oorro dwirro torra – right turn
chwarro dwirro torra –
        left turn
jumbi – ready stance

TAEKWONDO TENETS

Every dojang has rules about how to act that have to be followed. For example, students are expected to sit cross-legged with their backs straight when listening to their instructor! Behaviour in taekwondo is based on five tenets, or principles:

Courtesy (ye ui) – to act politely and kindly to others.
Integrity (yom chi) – to be honest with yourself and others at all times.
Perseverance (in nee) – to be loyal and patient when learning and not to give up.
Self-control (guk gi) – to keep calm and have control of your actions and emotions both inside and outside the dojang.
Indomitable spirit (baekjul boolgool) – to have a never-give-up attitude and to act correctly at all times.

An instructor takes a class through a warm-up, starting with loosening exercises, such as star jumps (far left), to increase the heart rate. Stretches (left) will prepare muscles for the activity ahead and help to increase flexibility.

9

STANCES

Taekwondo movements begin from a starting position known as a stance (or sogi in Korean). There are many different stances, but all put you in a balanced position ready to move suddenly in a number of directions.

DIFFERENT USES

The first stance you will learn is the ready stance. It is the starting point to move into other stances and is also used when performing patterns. Each of the stances has many different names, and is suited to a different situation. For example, the sitting stance (see page 11) places your legs wide apart with your knees bent as if you are sitting. It forms a stable base and is useful when learning punches. However, it is hard to change quickly out of this stance into another. This means that it is rarely used in sparring (see pages 24–25), when you need to move rapidly. Many stances have your weight balanced equally over both feet. The rear foot stance (see page 11) is unusual because almost all of your weight is placed over your back foot. This makes it easy for you to keep your balance as you perform kicks with your front foot.

Ready stance

This student is standing in the ready stance, with feet apart and fists in front of his hips.

Walking stance

1 Starting in the ready stance, the student steps forwards with his right foot and pulls his right fist back.

2 As he puts his right foot down, he pulls his left fist back and punches forwards with his right fist, twisting his body.

3 With the right foot planted, the right fist is extended and the left fist pulled back to the hip. The wide stance gives a solid base.

1 Having started in the ready stance, the student pulls his fists to the right, twists his body sideways and sweeps his right foot to the side to take a step back.

2 As he plants his right foot back, he pulls his fists up in front of his body.

3 The student holds his left fist out in front of him and his right fist against his chest to protect his body.

STANCE CLASS

Stances are practised over and over again as they help you build up control of different parts of your body and improve your balance. In sparring, competitors move quickly from one stance to another. For example, they may spend only a fraction of a second in a defensive back stance, before moving into a forward stance to launch an attack.

This stance is called guburyo sogi. The left fist is held out in front of the student and the right fist against the chest. All of the student's weight is on her right foot, while her left leg has been raised where it can protect the lower body or perform a quick snap kick (see pages 16–17).

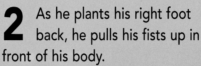

In the sitting stance, the feet are placed wide apart to provide a stable base.

In the rear foot stance, most of the weight is on the back foot, while the heel of the front foot is held off the ground.

11

SIMPLE STRIKES

Punches and hand strikes are an important part of taekwondo training, but the rules about them depend on which organisation you follow. Only body punches are allowed in WTF competitions, while punches and hand strikes to the head are allowed in ITF competitions.

BASIC PUNCHES

A punch is a hand strike made with a closed hand shaped into a fist. Making a good fist in taekwondo not only stops you injuring your hand, but it also transfers more of the energy from your punch into the target. A medium straight punch is aimed into the body, while a high straight punch is angled upwards and targets the head. In both cases, the aim is to make contact with the first two knuckles of your hand. This is because these are the two largest and strongest knuckles. As your punch connects, you twist your hand at the wrist. This helps you snap into the punch.

Punching tips

The power and accuracy of a good punch comes from all the parts of your body working together, including your shoulder, wrist and fist. Keep your arm and wrist relaxed until just before the moment of impact.

Making a fist

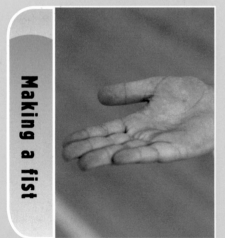

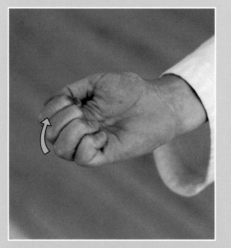

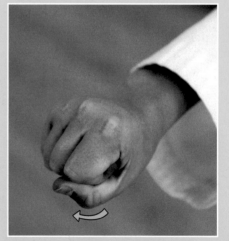

1 To make a fist correctly, start by holding out your hand, palm upwards, with your fingers extended and held together.

2 Roll your fingers into the palm of your hand, making sure that you clench them to keep the fist as tight as possible.

3 Finally, close the thumb around the knuckles of your fingers. You should always keep your thumb outside the fist, otherwise you risk breaking it.

1 This student is about to punch with her right hand. She pulls her left, non-punching, hand in the opposite direction.

2 Pulling the non-punching hand back twists her body into the punch and adds more power to the blow.

KNIFE HAND AND PALM HEEL

There are other shapes and parts of the hand apart from the fist that you can use to make a strike. These include the knife hand and the palm heel strikes. The knife hand strike uses the outside edge of your hand, between your wrist and the base of your little finger, to make contact. The palm heel strike is used to target the head or chin. The hand is pulled back, with the fleshy part of the palm connecting with the target.

The heel of the palm can be used to strike with the hand open and the fingers extended (top) or with the hand closed and the fingers slightly curled in (bottom).

The knife hand strike is made using a chopping action of the arm, bringing the side of the hand into contact with the target.

BLOCKS

Blocks allow you to stop or deflect the moving leg or arm of an opponent. The aim with all blocks is to stop the opponent's foot or hand from reaching its target.

STOPPING THREATS

Blocks are important both in self-defence, when they can stop a painful blow, and in competitions, when they stop an opponent scoring points. There are many different blocks. Each is designed to stop certain types of attack from an opponent, whether it is a punch aimed at the head or a kick to the body.

Low block

1 To perform a low block, the student begins by standing in the ready stance.

2 She pulls her arms up and to her right and starts to step forwards with her left foot.

3 As she plants her left foot, she brings her left hand down. Low blocks are used to stop kicks (see inset).

Inner forearm

1 To perform the inner forearm block, the student begins by standing in the ready stance.

2 She pulls her arms across to her left and starts to take a step forwards with her right foot.

3 As she plants her right foot, she brings her right arm back across her body. Inward blocks are used to stop body and head punches.

1 To perform a rising block, the student begins by standing in the ready stance.

2 He crosses his arms in front of him and starts to take a step forwards with his right foot.

3 As he plants his right foot, he sweeps his right arm upwards. Rising blocks are used to stop an overhead attack (see inset).

REACTION ARM

Blocks will fail if they are not made decisively and with speed and power. One way of increasing the speed and power of a block is with the reaction arm. This is where, as your blocking arm travels in one direction, you throw the arm you are not using to block in the opposite direction.

A cross fist pressing block is made by crossing the arms and pushing them downwards. It is used to block low kicks (see bottom).

A cross fist rising block is made by crossing the arms and pushing them upwards. It is used to block punches to the head (see right).de

SIMPLE KICKS

Taekwondo is best known for its wide range of different kicks. While flying kicks are the most spectacular, students start by learning kicks made with their non-kicking foot firmly on the ground.

WORKING BOTH LEGS

Kicks in taekwondo use many parts of your body, not just your feet and lower legs. For example, with a front snap kick, your knee must be lifted high and your hip twisted into the kick. You need all of your body's parts working together, which is why students practise each kick dozens of times. Being able to kick with either leg gives you more options when sparring.

Front snap kick

1 To start a front snap kick, the student stands in a walking stance with her feet wide apart.

2 She brings her right leg forwards and up sharply, bending her knee so that her leg is at right angles.

3 She then straightens her right leg with a sharp movement to deliver the kick.

4 Once the kick has been delivered, she quickly pulls her right leg back, bending at the knee, so that the leg is bent at right angles.

5 Finally, the kicking leg is brought back and down to the ground so that it returns to the starting position.

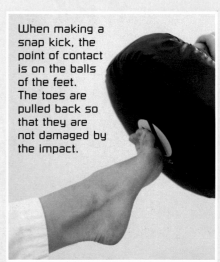

When making a snap kick, the point of contact is on the balls of the feet. The toes are pulled back so that they are not damaged by the impact.

16

1 To start a side snap kick, the student stands in a walking stance with her feet wide apart.

2 She brings her right leg up and forwards and twists her body so that it is sideways to the intended target.

3 To deliver the kick, the right leg is straightened quickly before being pulled back and down to the starting position.

1 To start a back kick, the student stands in a walking stance with her feet wide apart.

2 She raises her right kicking leg and pivots on her left standing leg so that her back is facing the intended target.

3 She continues to pivot on her left leg until she is sideways on to her target before extending her right leg to deliver the kick.

Kick tips

A natural mistake to make when you start to learn kicks is to lean your body backwards to balance out your kicking leg going forwards. As your kicking foot hits its target, this can unbalance you and knock you over. Try to lean forwards into a kick instead. This will improve your balance and help generate extra power.

4 Once the kick has been delivered, the right leg is pulled back and the student pivots back to the starting position.

17

ADVANCED KICKS

As you progress, your instructor will introduce you to more advanced kicks. Some of these, like the chopping movement of the axe kick, require you to stretch your leg above your head. Others, like the roundhouse kick, require quick yet smooth turning body movements.

SNAP BACK

How you finish a kick is very important. You should not just let your foot drop to the ground after making a kick. This can leave you unbalanced and open to attack. Instead, you should pull your leg back quickly into the correct stance. This leaves you ready to either defend an opponent's attack or to launch another kick.

Foot striking areas

Different kicks use different parts of the foot. Front snap kicks use the ball of the foot (1), while axe kicks use the heel (2). Some kicks use the outer ridge of the foot, known as the foot sword (3).

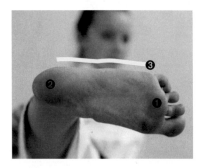

Jump kick

1 The student stands in the walking stance, but this time with her kicking leg forwards.

4 The right leg is extended sharply to deliver the kick.

2 She raises her non-kicking leg and bends her right, kicking leg ready to jump into the air.

3 Once in the air, she raises her right leg to start the kick, while bringing her left, non-kicking leg downwards.

5 She lands on her left leg and brings her right leg back and down to return to the starting position.

1 Starting in the walking stance, the student brings her right, kicking leg up and forwards in a circular motion, while twisting her body.

2 As she continues to pivot on her left leg, the kicking leg continues to come round, with the knee bent.

3 Once the student is sideways to the target, the right leg is extended sharply to deliver the kick.

WHICH KICK?

Working out which kick to use in a situation comes with practice and experience. In a split second, you will need to be able to figure out the distance to your opponent, what direction they are moving in and what would be the best kick to make from your current position and stance. As your legs are longer than your arms, kicks allow you to keep an opponent away from you. This means that certain kicks are good for defence as well as attack. Sometimes, though, your opponent may be too close to make certain kicks. You may have to change stance or move backwards or to the side to regain a position from which you can launch a kick.

4 With the kick delivered, the right leg is pulled back, round and downwards to return to the starting position.

1 The student starts in the ready position, before stepping back with the kicking leg and moving the arms out.

2 The right, kicking leg is then brought forwards and the right arm is raised above the head to help with the action.

3 The right arm is lowered as the right leg is raised above the head and then brought down sharply to deliver the kick.

ATTACK AND DEFENCE

Kicks, strikes and blocks are first taught separately. As your experience builds, you will learn to string two or three attacking moves together quickly and powerfully. These series of moves are known as combinations.

MAKING ATTACKS

Combinations can include a mixture of hand and foot strikes or several kicks in a row. A common combination pair of kicks is to perform a front snap kick with one leg and then turn your body to perform a side kick with your other leg. Some combinations start with a low kick, which may force the opponent to perform a low block. This can leave the opponent's head and chest area unguarded, so a second, higher kick or punch can hit its target.

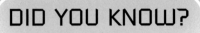

Block/punch

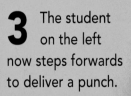

1 Here, the attacker on the right is about to deliver a punch with his right hand. The student on the left is preparing to block.

2 Having had his punch blocked, the student on the right is now exposed to a quick attack.

3 The student on the left now steps forwards to deliver a punch.

4 As she plants her right foot, she delivers a punch to the head.

20

1 Here, the attacker on the right is about to punch with his right hand. The student on the left is preparing to block.

2 With the punch blocked, the student on the left can now counter-attack.

3 She chooses to counter-attack with a roundhouse kick, lifting her left leg and spinning round to deliver a kick to the head.

STANCES AND DEFENCE

When fighting an opponent, a taekwondo competitor moves smoothly between different stances looking to launch attacks. Competitors use quick movements in defence to avoid a punch or kick hitting them – a skill called evasion. When making a kick, a competitor tries to keep his or her arms and fists in a position that forms a guard, able to defend and perform a block should the opponent launch a counter-attack.

Sometimes, the simplest form of defence is to take yourself out of the attacker's range. Here, the student on the right has spotted a kick. He has stepped back and to one side, taking himself out of range of the kick so that he cannot be hit.

WORKING ON PATTERNS

All taekwondo students will learn various patterns. These are long series of punches, kicks and blocks that are also known as tul or poomse in Korean. Patterns are designed to teach students how to deal with attacks coming from different directions and angles.

PATTERN PRACTICE

A taekwondo instructor takes his or her students through the movements of a pattern, demonstrating each stage for the students to follow. Each movement must be performed with speed and power, but also as precisely as possible because students should end patterns standing in the same spot as where they started. The movements in a pattern have to be remembered and practised frequently so that they flow smoothly. Even after mastering advanced patterns, top taekwondo students will still work on more basic patterns.

DIFFERENT SCHOOLS

There are many different series of patterns, depending on what school or style of taekwondo you perform. In WTF taekwondo, the set of patterns is called Taegeuk Poomse. In ITF taekwondo, there are 24 official patterns, one for each hour of the day. These increase in complexity and in the number of moves that the students have to perform. For example, the more complex So San pattern has an incredible 72 different movements.

Chon-Ji
This is the first pattern that beginners learn. It consists of 19 different movements and is made up of lots of low and medium height blocks and punches. It does not contain any kicks.

Dan-Gun
Named after the legendary founder of Korea, this pattern has 21 moves. As with Chon-Ji, it does not contain any kicks, but it does have high blocks.

Do-San
This is a slightly more complex pattern involving 24 moves. It also introduces kicks as well as more complicated types of block.

PATTERNS IN COMPETITION

Competitions are held for individuals, pairs or teams all performing the same patterns at the same time. Competitors' efforts are marked out of ten by a panel of judges who are looking for each movement within a pattern to be performed with accuracy, speed, power and rhythm. The judges remove 0.1 points from the score for each movement within a pattern that they feel the competitors did not perform accurately or with enough skill.

Patterns are rehearsed and performed in classes by students all at the same time. The teacher calls out instructions.

SPARRING

Sparring is the performing of stances, punches, blocks and kicks with another person. Called kyorugi in Korean, it is an excellent way of perfecting some of the skills you have already practised on your own or in classes.

NO CONTACT

Many taekwondo schools only allow sparring where no contact is made. Students control all of their kicks and hand strikes so that they stop short of an opponent. This includes step sparring, where the two students agree which moves are performed in advance. This allows the attacker to work on kicks and hand strikes while the defender, knowing which move is coming, can practise blocks and evasion skills.

SEMI-FREE AND FREE SPARRING

Semi-free sparring is usually no contact and with one student attacking and one defending. Unlike step sparring, though, the attacker can pick an attack without the defender knowing. Free full contact sparring is a sparring contest under close control of an instructor where students wear protective clothing.

No pressure

No taekwondo student should ever be forced to spar if they do not want to. If you are nervous, talk to your instructor. Remember that a good taekwondo school usually makes sure that sparring is performed between students of similar sizes and abilities.

DID YOU KNOW?

Each colour belt has a different meaning in taekwondo. White means innocence while green represents growth – the growing of a student's taekwondo skills.

In this fighting stance, the student is using a guarding block with her right forearm to protect herself against the attacker's strikes.

1 These students are step sparring, using pre-selected moves to practise their technique. The student on the right has blocked a punch.

2 She then delivers her own punch to the head, but without connecting. The students then return to the starting position to repeat the move.

SPARRING SAFETY

Whatever the type of sparring, there are certain rules that are always followed. These include never wrestling an opponent or grabbing hold of his or her arms or legs. Sparring is a great test not only of your physical taekwondo skills, speed and fitness, but also of your character. Students need to hold back strikes so that they stop short and do not harm a fellow student.

These students are sparring during a class. They are wearing padded protective gear and are sparring under the supervision of their instructor.

GRADING AND BREAKING

When an instructor believes you are ready, you may get the chance to sit a grading exam. This exam tests your taekwondo skill and knowledge, allowing you to move up the different ranks or levels in taekwondo. These levels are known as kups.

GRADING

Grading tests or exams vary depending on which taekwondo school you visit. Usually, though, grading involves a student performing a number of basic stances, blocks, punches and kicks and certain patterns in front of one or more examiners. The student may also be asked questions about facts they have learned in their classes, such as the five tenets of taekwondo (see page 9).

MOVING UP THE BELTS

If a student passes a grading exam, he or she will receive a new belt which is colour-coded to show the kup a student has reached. There are 10 kups, starting with a white belt or 10th kup for a total beginner up to a red belt with a black stripe called a tab for the 1st kup (see page 27). Above these levels are black belts for advanced taekwondo practitioners.

(see page 9)

(see page 27)

DID YOU KNOW?

In 2008, Rohullah Nikpai won Afghanistan's first ever Olympic medal when he defeated two-time world champion Juan Antonio Ramos to win the bronze medal in the flyweight taekwondo competition. The Afghan government gave Nikpai a house as a prize!

These students are taking part in a grading exam. They are carrying out a set sequence of moves and patterns and they are being marked, or graded, by an examiner.

BREAKING

Breaking or destruction, from the Korean word, gyokpa, is the use of taekwondo kicks and hand strikes to break materials, often wooden boards. These can be spectacular demonstrations of power and timing but they are also used in some taekwondo schools to help condition students and test the strength and timing of their moves. Competitions are held for breaking. In ITF competitions, wooden boards that are 1.5 centimetres (0.6 inches) thick are used.

Kups

10th kup	White belt
9th kup	White belt with yellow tabs
8th kup	Yellow belt
7th kup	Yellow belt with green tabs
6th kup	Green belt
5th kup	Green belt with blue tabs
4th kup	Blue belt
3rd kup	Blue belt with red tabs
2nd kup	Red belt
1st kup	Red belt with black tabs

Taekwondo students are taught to deliver a sharp yell called a kihap when they make a punch or kick. It can help to channel a student's energy and breathing into a blow, gaining maximum power. Sometimes, it can also frighten or unsettle an opponent.

COMPETITION TAEKWONDO

While competitions for breaking and performing patterns exist, the most well-known taekwondo competitions are for sparring between pairs of contestants. These contests are held at local level right up to the World Taekwondo Championships, which takes place every two years.

MAJOR COMPETITIONS

Taekwondo appears at many multi-sport events, including the Pan-American Games and the Asian Games. Different competitions have different rules. For example, ITF events allow hand strikes to the head whereas WTF rules do not. ITF competitors do not wear a chest protector but do wear padded footwear and gloves.

OLYMPIC TAEKWONDO

Taekwondo first appeared at the Olympics as a demonstration sport in 1988 and a full medal sport in 2000. It follows WTF rules, with four weight divisions each for men and women. The action takes place inside a square contest area and consists of three rounds, each three minutes long for men and two minutes long for women. Competitors wear protection including shinpads, a mouthguard, a padded headguard and a padded trunk protector, called a hogu, that wraps round the body. Under WTF rules, hand strikes must be made with a closed fist.

Competition area

Taekwondo competitions take place inside a square court measuring 8 metres (26 feet) across. Around this is an area called the safety boundary, which measures at least 2 metres (6.5 feet) wide. Judges sit in each of the corners, while a referee can move around inside the contest area. At the start of a bout, the competitors stand in the centre, 2 metres (6.5 feet) apart and opposite each other.

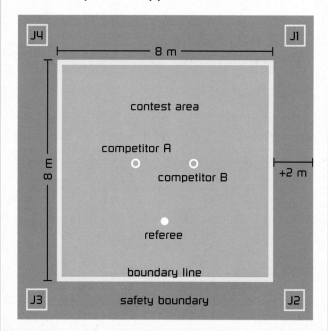

J4 • J1 • 8 m • contest area • competitor A • competitor B • 8 m • +2 m • referee • boundary line • J3 • safety boundary • J2

1 At the start of a bout, the referee invites the competitors into the court.

2 The referee then instructs the competitors to bow to each other.

3 The referee then steps forwards with his arm extended between the two competitors. When he pulls this arm back, the bout begins.

4 At the end of the bout, the referee declares the winner by raising that fighter's arm.

5 The two competitors then shake hands.

In a competition, one fighter will wear blue protective gear. That fighter is known by the Korean word Chung. The other fighter will wear red protective gear. That fighter is known by the Korean word Hong.

POINTS SCORING

In Olympic taekwondo, a judge sits at each corner of the contest area, and they decide if a strike is legal, accurate and made with enough force. If three of the four judges agree, a competitor will gain one point for a strike to the trunk protector with either the fist or foot and two points if a kick strikes the face of the opponent. Points can also be deducted if a competitor commits a foul, such as striking an opponent who is on the floor, wrestling an opponent or using a knee or elbow. If scores are equal after three rounds in a final, a fourth, sudden-death round is held to determine the winner.

GLOSSARY AND RESOURCES

Glossary

block A taekwondo move that stops or deflects an opponent's attack.

breaking The part of taekwondo dealing with competitors or students using a strike with the hands or feet to break wooden boards or other materials.

chung In a sparring competition, the Korean word for the competitor wearing blue.

contest area The square marking the limits of a competition arena.

counter-attack An attack made in response to an opponent's attack.

courtesy Polite and considerate ways of acting towards other people.

dobok A taekwondo uniform.

dojang The Korean word for a martial arts hall or gymnasium.

focus pads Pads worn on the hand by one person so that another person can practise their punches and kicks.

hogu The Korean word for a padded chest protector worn by competitors in bouts.

hong The competitor in a sparring competition wearing red.

ITF Short for the International Taekwondo Federation, a major organising body of taekwondo.

kup A grade showing a student's level of ability in taekwondo.

kyorugi The Korean word for sparring.

martial art A system of practices and traditions used for training for combat. Martial arts include taekwondo, judo and karate.

patterns A sequence of movements in taekwondo carried out in a precise way.

referee An official in charge of a taekwondo sparring competition.

sogi The Korean word for stance, or the position in which a person stands.

sparring A contest using taekwondo skills to strike an opponent. Most sparring is practice work, often with the moves agreed beforehand.

sudden-death A fourth round added to a taekwondo bout when the scores are level. The first person to score a point in the extra round is considered to be the winner.

tenets Principles or ways of behaving. Behaviour in taekwondo is based on five tenets.

tul The Korean word for patterns used in ITF taekwondo.

WTF Short for the World Taekwondo Federation, one of the two biggest international organisations running taekwondo.

Diet and nutrition

Taekwondo demands total focus, with all your energy concentrated into making quick, accurate movements whether in training or in a competition. Eating poorly with a diet containing lots of fatty foods and sugar, can leave you tired and lacking the concentration, speed and balance you need to perform at your best. A healthy diet contains plenty of nutrients from foods such as fresh fruit and vegetables, lean meats, chicken and fish, pasta, rice and pulses. These help provide the vitamins and minerals your body needs for growth and repair as well as providing energy for you to perform.

At a taekwondo tournament, competitors normally take part in a number of bouts. These are not usually at set times, so you need to top up your energy levels straight after one bout with healthy snacks such as cereal bars, fresh or dried fruits, or a small sandwich. Eating small amounts gives your body time to start digesting and turning the food into energy before you approach your next bout.

Although a taekwondo contest may last only a few minutes, all your efforts can cause a lot of fluid loss from your body in the form of sweat. Look to top up your fluids by taking small but regular sips of water or juice. Avoid fizzy drinks as these can make you feel bloated when competing or training.

http://www.olympics.org.uk/chillzone/rightstuffs-port.aspx?sp=TK&se=diet
A great page on diet and nutrition for taekwondo at the British Olympics website.

http://www.eatwell.gov.uk/healthydiet/foodfor-sport/sportnexercise/
A really useful article on healthy eating for active sports like taekwondo.

Resources

http://www.itftkd.org
http://www.itf-administration.com
http://www.tkd-itf.org
These three websites represent the three bodies that now make up the International Taekwondo Federation.

http://www.wtf.org/
The homepage of the World Taekwondo Federation.

http://www.talktaekwondo.co.uk/
A great website with lots of information on all different aspects of taekwondo.

http://www.britishtaekwondo.org.uk/
Homepage of the British Taekwondo Control Board. The website has galleries of action photos and a handy find-a-club feature to locate taekwondo classes and schools in your area.

http://www.wustaekwondo.com/techniques/technique-home.htm
This website contains lots of information and pictures of stances, kicks and other techniques. It also features diagrams of patterns and links to videos.

http://www.ir.isas.jaxa.jp/~cpp/TKD/technique/blocks-e.html#TOP
A useful webpage all about blocking techniques, with pictures and videos.

http://www.taekwondo-network.com/
This website contains short features on all aspects of taekwondo, from techniques and competitions to the history and philosophy of the martial art.

INDEX